Steven David Catlin, Serial Killer

Ruth Kanton

Published by Trellis Publishing, 2021.

STEVEN DAVID CATLIN, SERIAL KILLER

First edition. July 5, 2021.

ISBN: 979-8224274642

Written by Ruth Kanton.

STEVEN DAVID CATLIN, SERIAL KILLER

1

RUTH CANTON

Steven David Catlin

Born in 1944, Steven David Catlin was adopted as an infant by a couple living in Kern County, California. Martha and Glenn Catlin took in the child and treated him as their own, making sure that he was well taken care of to the best of their ability. However, they soon found that their son's personality was a bit removed from the norm, and tried their best to help him find his footing in the world. Martha was a doting mother, and loved Catlin to a fault. By the early 1950s, the family had moved to Bakersfield, 40 miles north of Los Angeles. As he entered his teenage years, Catlin became more and more unwilling to conform to the societal norms present, choosing to find his own path. His parents were finding it impossible to keep him in line, or even convince him to follow a straight path. He began shunning school, and was unwilling to involve himself in anything related to his education. While it seemed logical that he find a job to support himself because he wasn't interested in school, Catlin refused to do it. He despised doing any form of work, and started to do drugs. By 1960, Catlin was always either high on drugs or looking to find money to score more drugs. School began fading further and further into the background, and he finally opted to drop out. He maintained that school was not for him. This, coupled with his drug addiction, made him more desperate to fund his drug habit. Not willing to find a job, he began forging checks. He was finally arrested, and was sentenced to 40 weeks at a California Youth Authority camp in 1963.

Marriages and Divorces

Catlin met his first wife after his release from the camp. However, he was abusive to his wife, and his drug use was getting worse. The domestic problems that plagued the marriage starting taking their toll on his wife, and she chose to leave him. Soon after she left, Catlin began seeing someone else, and in 1966, chose to marry her without seeking a divorce from his first wife. He used a pseudonym on his birth certificate, and seemed to be in no particular hurry to get a divorce. However, just a few months into his second marriage, Catlin was arrested after he stole a credit card to finance his drug habit. During his sentencing, the judge stated that he was a drug addict and gave him a three-year sentence to be served at a state prison in Chino. After his release from prison, he finally decided to do right by his second wife. He sought a divorce and legally married his second wife using his real name. However, after his release from prison, the relationship only lasted for ten months before the couple decided to separate. Soon after his third marriage ended, Catlin once again began a relationship with his soon-to-be third wife, Edith Ballew. The relationship did not fare any better compared to his previous marriages, and the two separated after only eight months of marriage. Ballew kept an interest in her former husband's affairs even after their separation and subsequent divorce.

Joyce Adeline Catlin

After his marriage to Ballew ended, Catlin began Joyce Adeline, an employee of the welfare department in the local authority. During the marriage, Catlin worked as a garage hand or in service stations. His need to make more money had him looking for ways to accomplish this dream, but his reality was far from ideal. He was always strapped for cash, and his menial jobs ensured that he would not be breaking bank for a long period of time. His marriage to Adeline, who changed her name to Joyce Catlin after the marriage, lasted longer than his relationship with Ballew. However, sometime in April 1976, Adeline went to a physician complaining of flu-like symptoms. After the initial examination, the physician recommended that she be admitted in hospital. She complained of vomiting, back pain, and a sore throat. The day after she was admitted, Adeline was transferred to the intensive care unit. It seemed like her lungs had been infected, and Dr. Einstein, a lung specialist, was called in to consult. Suspecting that she had either a bacterial or viral infection, Dr. Einstein began administering treatment, but no progress was noted. After a few days, her lungs were barely able to oxygenate her body effectively, and she was put on mechanical ventilation. She did not respond to any of the antibiotics provided, and nineteen days after she was admitted, Joyce Catlin died on May 6, 1976. She was 40 years old at the time. Her death certificate listed the cause of death as acute respiratory failure due to an unknown microorganism.

Catlin chose to have her body cremated soon after her death.

Glenn Catlin

A year after Adeline's death, Catlin met Glenna Kaye in May 1977, and the two got married. Having garnered extensive experience while working with Glendon Emery's pit crew while he was married to Adeline, Catlin found a job in a garage based in Fresno, California. The couple promptly moved to the new location, and Catlin was able to showcase his skills in the garage. Catlin knew his way around cars, and his talents were obvious to everyone working in the garage, including his superiors. His efforts and skills were soon appreciated, and he was promoted to a managerial position and placed in charge of 40 employees. As his position in the company rose, Catlin did not see any favorable changes in his financial position. He had expensive tastes, and he was strapped for cash.

On October 28, 1980, Glenn Catlin suddenly died. A medical examination revealed that his lungs were filled with fluid, but no foul play was suspected. It was concluded that his death was caused by his lung cancer. Catlin quickly had his father's body cremated, and pocketed the finances that became available after his death. Catlin burned through the inheritance in record time, and he found himself exactly where he had started – broke.

As time moved on, Catlin became more desperate for cash, prompting his to begin stealing from his employers. He stole various automotive parts, progressing from the cheaper parts to the more expensive ones. As the expensive parts began disappearing, his employers started noticing. There were no apparent suspects, and an investigation did not reveal anyone with a motive. Unsure of what to do next, the employers decided to carry out a background check on all the employees. It did not take long for them to uncover Catlin's criminal past, and they confronted him. Catlin was offered a way out. He would resign, and no charges would be filed against him. He quickly accepted.

Glenna Kaye Catlin

On February 17, 1984, Glenna Kaye Catlin prepared to take a trip to Las Vegas with her mother. They had been planning this mother-daughter holiday for a while, and the excitement was insurmountable. Soon after they arrived at their destination, Kaye began complaining to her mother that she was not feeling well. Her condition made her so uncomfortable that they promptly cut the trip short on the same day and traveled back to Fresno. She went to hospital for medical examination, but the doctors were unable to give her any answers. She was hospitalized for observation, and doctors began trying to make sense of Kaye's illness. They finally maintained that she had fluid in her lungs, and they listed this as their official diagnosis. For 22 days, doctors spent their time trying to figure out why Kaye was sick, and she finally died on March 14, 1984. The hospital kept samples of Kaye's tissues for future analysis, hoping to solve the mystery once the technological advances made it possible. Kaye had a life insurance policy worth $58,785, and Catlin was the sole beneficiary of the amount.

While visiting Kaye in hospital, Catlin met Carol Johnson, and the two quickly got engaged.

Martha Catlin

Following their divorce, Catlin's third wife had been closely following his life, monitoring any unusual events. In 1982, Martha Catlin suffered a stroke, but Ballew did not believe that it was due to natural causes. She called Martha's physician, Dr. Sproule, and suggested that Martha may have been poisoned using paraquat. After his examination, Dr. Sproule concluded that there had been no sign of poisoning. Ballew was not convinced, but she did not push the issue further. In September 1984, Martha once again paid Dr. Sproule a visit, this time revealing that she was not taking her hypertension medicine as prescribed. Consequently, she was experiencing high blood pressure.

A month later, on October 31, she made another visit to the physician's office, this time complaining of poor memory and poor eating habits. She told the doctor that she had been drinking wine despite being ordered to avoid alcohol while on medication. Dr. Sproule then prescribed cough syrup with codeine.

Aware of her former mother-in-law's health problems, Ballew paid Martha a visit on November 29, 1984. She noted that Martha was her usual self, and seemed healthy at the time. A week later, on December 6, Martha called her friend and reported that she was feeling seriously ill. When Anna Stonebraker made it to Martha's house, she noticed that her friend seemed very ill, and had purple swollen lips and mouth. Martha had dark circles under her eyes. Mrs. Stonebraker took Martha back to Dr. Sproule's office, who took note of the purple reddish lips and throat, and recorded her temperature at 102 degrees. He prescribed penicillin and asked Martha to come back the next day. When Mrs. Stonebraker revealed that she wouldn't be able to take care of her friend the next day, she called Catlin and left a message asking him to come to his mother's house the next day. He called back later, telling them that he wouldn't be able to drive to Bakersfield the next day. Catlin then called Dr. Sproule the next day and promised to send someone to take care of Martha. On December 7, 1984, Mrs. Stonebraker and Martha arrived at Dr. Sproule's office. He noted that Martha's throat was still purplish, and her throat was sore. She also had trouble eating. He wasn't alarmed, and sent her home to continue with her medication. The next morning at 5:30 a.m., he received a call from Martha's house. The caller informed him that Martha appeared to be dead, and he sent an ambulance to the residence. Martha Catlin was pronounced dead on arrival. She was 79 years old at the time.

The possible cause of death was listed as stroke, but the hospital needed to perform an autopsy to confirm. Catlin seemed eager to get his mother's body cremated, but the cremation was delayed until an autopsy could be performed. The pathologist responsible for her autopsy,

Dr. Dollinger, took tissue samples from Martha's lungs and kidneys for further analysis. He refused to list a cause of death until he received the results from the lab.

Suspicion

After learning about Martha's death on December 9, Ballew called Martha's house in Bakersfield. Catlin picked up the phone and informed her that his mother had died after exhibiting flu-like symptoms. Ballew, who had been following Catlin's life after their divorce, did not buy into his explanation about his mother's death. She believed that her ex-husband was somehow responsible for his mother's deaths, as well as the deaths of his fourth and fifth wives. Ballew was inclined to believe that one death connected to Catlin had a genuine cause, but four deaths in eight years, that was definitely suspicious. Tired of keeping her suspicions to herself, she made her way to the local sheriff's department. After presenting her suspicions, the sheriff was not sure that there was even enough evidence to warrant an investigation.

After completing Martha's autopsy, Dr. Dollinger sent the tissue samples to a Chevron laboratory in Richmond. The samples were analyzed by Dr. Ford, a clinical toxicologist at the lab. In his final report, Dr. Ford stated that Martha had ingested a substantial amount of paraquat. He sent his report to Dr. Dollinger, who subsequently listed Martha's cause of death as paraquat poisoning. With this report, investigators were finally called in to determine whether Martha had ingested the paraquat willingly or if she was a victim of foul play. With no tissue sample from Glenn's body, investigators decided to work with what they had. They interviewed medical personnel who attended to Joyce Adeline and Glenna Kaye, Catlin's wives who had died with eerily similar symptoms.

Unknown to Catlin, nurses and doctors attending to Adeline had suspected that she may have been suffering from paraquat poisoning, but there was no way to prove their suspicions. The medical examiner also had a similar suspicion, but at the time, there was no test for paraquat poisoning. He had secretly taken samples of Adeline's body tissues and stored them, hoping that one day there would be the right technology to test for paraquat. Investigators also spoke to Kaye's doctors and nurses, who quickly informed them that the medical examiner had taken tissue samples from her body. Investigators sent the tissue samples from Adeline and Kaye to the lab in Richmond to determine whether paraquat poisoning may have contributed to their deaths. Just like Martha's results, it was evident that Adeline and Kaye had both been poisoned by paraquat shortly before their deaths. It was clear to investigators that Ballew's suspicions had been warranted.

Motive(s)

Investigators were convinced that Catlin may have been responsible for the murders of his two wives and mother, but needed to find a motive. Pretty quickly, it became clear that the murders may have been financially motivated. After he was fired from his position at the Fresno garage, Catlin financial situation became dire, and his menial jobs were not enough to cover his expensive tastes. Adeline had a credit life insurance which was used to pay her $6,741 automobile debt, an insurance policy that paid a maximum of $2,000, and a $5,000 life insurance policy. Catlin was the sole beneficiary. The investigators were also made aware of Kaye's $56,785 life insurance payout to Catlin. In Martha's case, investigators discovered that Catlin was the sole beneficiary of her estate, but that she had been thinking of leaving it to the African Violet Society, a charity organization. According to various parties, Martha had not approved of her son's multiple marriages and divorces, and was contemplating removing him as her primary beneficiary. Additionally, a number of sources mentioned that Catlin had been getting tired of taking care of his elderly mother, and had made the statement that he wished she "would hurry up and die" on several occasions.

Investigators also found out that Catlin had been planning to move his mother from Bakersfield to Fresno, and that she had already asked him to look for a home in Fresno. Martha's bank revealed that in November 1984, Catlin and his mother had withdrawn money from her bank account intended as down payment for her new home in Fresno. Investigators discovered that Catlin had never used the money for its intended purpose, and that he still had the money in his possession. The financial motive was enough for authorities to arrest Catlin, and he was taken into custody on February 14, 1985.

1986 Sentencing

Prosecutors in Kern County were convinced that Catlin was responsible for the deaths of the three women, and subsequently brought three murder charges against him. In April 1986, his hearing for the murder of Kaye began in Monterey Superior County Court. Expert witnesses maintained that Kaye's death was definitely as a result of paraquat poisoning. Investigators testified that Catlin had access to the herbicide, having worked for an agricultural enterprise sometime in the 1970s. Authorities had recovered a bottle of paraquat in the garage where Catlin worked with his former father-in-law, Kaye's father. The bottle of paraquat had a 1977 date, and Catlin's fingerprint was found on the cap.

A number of witnesses maintained that Catlin's marriage to Kaye was that of convenience, and that he had been unfaithful to her during the marriage. A few days before she became sick, witnesses saw the couple arguing in public. According to a number of people, Kaye was jealous of Catlin's other partners. It was also revealed that in 1977, Catlin had spoken to Kaye's half-brother about the dangers of paraquat poisoning, specifically mentioning how paraquat damages the lungs. Other witnesses mentioned that during Kaye's funeral, Catlin seemed to have been grieving, but that his mood quickly lifted after the funeral was over. Coupled with the $56,785 insurance payout, the jury was convinced beyond a reasonable doubt that Catlin had indeed killed his fifth wife, Glenna Kaye Catlin.

The jury returned a guilty verdict, and on April 15, 1986 Catlin was sentenced to life without parole for the death of his wife.

1990 Sentencing

On September 7, 1988, prosecutors in Kern County amended the charges brought against Catlin for Adeline and Martha's murders to include his life sentence for the murder of Kaye. His charges were the first degree murder of Martha and first degree murder of Adeline, with special circumstances. The prosecutors added for special circumstances to the charges including; murder for financial gain, committing more than one first or second degree murder, intentional killing of a victim by administering poison, and being convicted of the first degree murder of Glenna Kaye Catlin. The trial began on April 23, 1990 in Kern County. Prosecutors chose to try Catlin for both the 1976 murder of Joyce Adeline Catlin and the 1984 murder of Martha Catlin in the same trial. The defense tried to get the trials to be separated, but the judge denied their request.

When put on the stand, Dr. Ford from the Chevron laboratory explained how paraquat poisoning progressed in the body. He explained that the victim would experience a burning sensation in the mouth followed by nausea, vomiting, and diarrhea 12 hours later. The symptoms would persist for a few days followed by kidney impairment which is resolved in 14 days. A week after infection, the lungs would be affected, and by three weeks, the lungs become so fibriotic that they fail to function. He explained that according to Adeline's physicians, these were the same symptoms she exhibited up until her death. The Medical Examiner of the City and County of San Francisco, Dr. Stephens, testified that he had reviewed Adeline's medical records and tissue slides, and found her symptoms consistent with paraquat poisoning. He maintained that it was his belief that this was the cause of her death. Witnesses mentioned that before Adeline began showing symptoms, she had attended a party and other attendees noted that she seemed intoxicated. The prosecution also highlighted the financial benefits that

Catlin obtained after Adeline's death. Catlin had been engaging in extramarital affairs while married to Adeline, and the two had argued about one of his girlfriends.

With regards to Catlin's access to paraquat, the prosecutors explained that he had worked at an agricultural enterprise as a mechanic in 1976 and 1976. Additionally, a number of witnesses revealed that Catlin was well aware of the effects of paraquat poisoning, since he had explained it to them on a number of occasions. The father of Catlin's second wife stated that Catlin had shown his a container of poison which he mentioned would be the most ideal for murder since it could not be detected and had no antidote. Adeline's son told the court that Catlin had warned him about entering the garage in 1985, cautioning him against the dangerous agricultural poisons present. He also added that Catlin had warned about coming into contact with paraquat. Ballew was also called to the stand, and she stated that after Adeline's death, she and a number of people had a feeling that Catlin was responsible. Perhaps the most damning evidence was that shortly after Adeline was admitted, Catlin brought her a milkshake, which many suspected had been laced with paraquat.

Dr. Ford also testified in Martha's case, stating that he believed she had ingested diluted paraquat a few days before her death. He also revealed that up until two to three years before the trial, Chevron was the sole distributor of paraquat in the United States. Dr. Killburn testified that Martha's lung damage was consistent with paraquat poisoning, which he believed she ingested around three to six days before her death. He maintained that her frail condition caused her to succumb to the poison before her lungs became highly fibriotic. Dr. Stephens testified that although it was possible that Martha may have died of a heart attack, he was convinced that she had died from paraquat poisoning. She was already exhibiting early signs of paraquat poisoning, and she had enough paraquat in her system to cause death. Prosecutors highlighted the expert witnesses' statements, who all believed that Martha's death was as a result of paraquat poisoning. Other witnesses stated that Martha had planned on removing Catlin as her sole beneficiary in favor of a charitable organization. Catlin was the only one listed in Martha's will, and he had pocketed money that was supposed to cater to the down payment of her new home in Fresno. Other witnesses stated that Catlin had expressed that he was tired of taking care of his mother, and was eagerly waiting for her demise, preferably sooner rather than later. Catlin had weekly or biweekly visits with his mother, and the prosecution stated that the week prior to Martha's death, Catlin had been mostly absent from work. However, the witnesses who gave this testimony later changed it, and testified that Catlin may have left for Bakersfield on either December 6 or 7, 1984. According to Catlin's fiancée at the time, the couple had driven to Martha's home on December 2, and he had not been left alone with his mother for any period of time during that visit. A bottle of paraquat was presented as evidence, and investigators testified that the poison had been recovered in the garage that Catlin shared with his former father-in-law, Kaye's father. On the cap, investigators found Catlin's fingerprint.

A jailhouse informant was put on the stand to testify against Catlin. He stated that Catlin had solicited him to intimidate Ballew, who the defense claimed had a vendetta against Catlin stemming from their broken relationship. The informant also revealed that Catlin had told him, "I killed the b***s." Catlin took the stand in his own defense, stating that he never told anyone that paraquat was an ideal murder weapon. He maintained his innocence, stating that the poison was found in an area in the garage that was designated to his former father-in-law. He also highlighted the fact that there were other people who had access to the garage. Catlin's credibility was brought into question when the prosecution highlighted his 1966 forgery conviction.

The jury was convinced that the prosecution had proven beyond a reasonable doubt that Catlin was responsible for the two murders. On June 1, 1990, the jury found Catlin guilty of the first degree murders of Adeline and Martha. They also found the first three of the special circumstance to be true. The penalty phase of the trial was set for June 5, 1990. On June 6, the same jury sentenced Catlin to serve life without parole for the murder of Joyce Adeline Catlin, and a death sentence for the murder of Martha Catlin. The jury also determined that the fourth special circumstance was true. This was because they were only made aware of Kaye's trial and verdict during the penalty phase of the trial.

Appeals

After his sentencing, Catlin filed numerous appeals with the California Supreme Court, and they were denied. In one appeal request, Catlin's lawyers maintained that the prosecution was in error for trying the two cases together. They explained that Adeline's case was the reason Catlin was sentenced to death for Martha's murder. Chief Justice Ronald M. George responded to the appeal request, maintaining that the joint trial was appropriate because of the similarities between the two cases. He also maintained that evidence from the Kaye murder was admissible because of the same reason.

Catlin is serving his time at San Quentin State Prison.

CHRIS WATTS

What is a perfect marriage?

Here is an interesting occupation – start typing 'What makes a perfect...?' and the predictive elements of the search engine you are using will rarely complete the question with the word 'marriage'. 'Day', 'teacher', 'occasion' and even 'tense' appear higher in the list. Is that a comment on how we live today, when a perfect marriage is seen as unobtainable to most couples?

Elements of the gutter press like to have their input into this problem. From time to time they will offer the latest crank study which will explain how to turn a marriage from a battleground into a palace of mutual adoration, pink heart shaped cushions and with the occasional dove fluttering by: such tips as saying 'I love you' ten times a week; going out on a date three times a month – quite how to find that number of baby sitters raises a question or two – is the sort of advice they typically offer. On a somewhat more serious scale, Global market researchers OnePoll.com recently asked a thousand Americans what, for them, constituted a perfect marriage.

The answers were not surprising; spontaneity, sharing interests, trust, talking honestly about deep and meaningful topics. But, Chris and Shanann Watts would seem to have had no need for either type of assistance in their marriage. They would not need to call upon the conclusions of others, or the psychoanalysis of those who claim to be experts in their field.

'Chris, we are so incredibly blessed to have you! You do so much every day for us and take such great care of us. You are the reason I was brave enough to agree to number 3. From Laundry to kids showers. You are incredible, and we are so lucky to have you in our life.'

Those were the words that Shanann wrote on her Facebook page, about her husband, for Fathers' Day. This was not an isolated incident, a one off attempt to be overtly public in a wife's display of love for her husband. Cynics might suggest that this, and other, messages could be seen as an unsubtle attempt to portray a marriage filled with happiness, when in fact it was littered with despair. But, no, Shanann's sentiments were genuine.

Because her husband Chris Watts was, to all intents and purposes, a terrific guy.

'He would reach out and help anybody,' said close family friend, Jeremy Lindstrom. 'He was a good mechanic, if you needed help with your car he would help you; if you needed help moving the furniture he'd be over in a heartbeat to help you out.'

Other friends described them as a perfect couple as well. And it was that kind of judgement which led Lindstrom to state, after news of the events of August 13th, that 'You know the worst thing of all when you are close to the family, the lie, the lie gets bigger.'

In fact, some six years previously Chris had made a well-received presentation to his college where he outlined the importance of sustaining relationships, and of getting through tough times. That too had been the cause of much admiration from Shanann.

Even more, the picture presented to friends and family, mostly from Shanann, was that a perfect relationship was soon to get even better. They had already been blessed with two gorgeous daughters, Bella (who was four) and her three-year-old sister Celeste. Next, in a few days, Shanann was hosting a special party.

She had already proudly posted an ultrasound image of their new child, with whom she was just over three months pregnant, on Facebook. At the party, she would announce the gender of the latest member of the Watts family. It was a boy, and they would call him Nico. The thirty-four-year-old wife, with the good job, the nice home, the terrific kids and the perfect, loving husband really did seem to have it all.

But, she didn't. It certainly seems to be the case that Shanann's publicly offered feelings were true to her heart, but her husband's were not. He was a man with many secrets; we are only just beginning to learn the extent of these, and time will help to identify those that are true, and those that have emerged, on shaky ground, from the gossip surrounding the tragic and horrific story which is about to unfold.

Because Chris Watts is currently in prison, awaiting trial on a number of charges. Among them, are the first-degree murders of Shanann, Celeste and Bella, along with causing the premature termination of his son's life.

The town of Frederick, Colorado, lies to the West of Rocky Mountains, thirty kilometers or so from the National Park which features the best of this beautiful Colorado landscape. The town is growing fast, with major building development programs seeing the population grow by 50% over the last eight years. Its current size means it is home to nearly 14000 inhabitants.

Chris and Shanann Watts were one of the newcomers to this town. Formerly a mining community, it carries the first name of its founders' father. Frederick has always attracted outsiders; when it first came into existence, at the turn of the twentieth century, immigrants from Europe and Latin America arrived, seeking their fortunes underground. The mine closed in the late twenties, and today the town serves as a dormitory for Denver, fifty kilometers to the South. It offers a gateway to the mountains, and its wide streets are frequently dressed in snow.

It is a lovely place to bring up a family. Perhaps it was that which attracted the young married Watts couple. They became wed in 2010. Originally, they hailed from North Carolina, but moved east to take up home in the small town which would witness the recent atrocities.

Shanann had a good job working for the nutritional company, Le-Vel. The global organization is a modern business; cloud based and claiming to be the fastest growing health and wellness organization in the world. It likes to be known as a *movement*, rather than a business. Shanann's employment there required her to travel from time to time. Chris too had a good job. He worked as an operator at the Anadarko Petroleum Corp based across the state.

But maybe there were hints that things were not as happy in the Watts household as the picture Shanann created. Family and friends are now racking their brains for clues, and slowly some are beginning to emerge. None are conclusive evidence in themselves of an unhappy marriage, but they offer just a little insight into what may have been happening at home. The murders are still painfully fresh for all, and in time no doubt more details will enter the public domain, but for now we take such clues as we have.

In the weeks before her murder, Shanann had posted a different kind of Facebook comment compared to her usual loving words. She had discovered one of her daughters' dolls sleeping on their sofa. The doll was propped up on two orange cushions, apparently at rest. What was disturbing was that the doll's face was covered by a toy sheet or handkerchief. It was as though she had died and been covered in the same way that a corpse's face is hidden.

'I do not know what to think of this,' she posted. Perhaps the covering of the face was purely coincidental, perhaps she had come across a game one of her girls was playing, possibly influenced by what she had seen on TV, and Shanann was simply putting an adult's perspective onto a child's game.

Some friends have suggested that the doll's presentation could have been a kind of macabre hint from Chris of what was going to happen. We do not know, although the doll's 'death' was an unusual discovery to make, and one which clearly caused some concern to Shanann, but not enough to raise any alarms.

Of more concrete concern is a fact that Shanann may, or may not, have been aware. Her husband was in debt, serious debt; in fact, debt to the tune of $70000. Could this have been a motivating force behind his crimes? Despite the insurance policies in place, the lives of four people, including his unborn son, at under $20000 each is hard to believe. Especially when these victims are his wife and children. He clearly loves his daughters. Numerous videos are online of him playing with the girls, like any other loving father. In one, his young daughter is captured singing about her father:

'My daddy is a hero, he helps me grow up strong,' she warbles in that slightly tuneless way of a young child. In another clip, Shanann cannot keep back her love for her husband: he is the 'best dad' anybody could wish for, she says.

However, some other evidence has come to light suggesting that Shanann may have become more uncertain about her future with Chris. Certain friends have claimed that Shanann expressed her concerns to them that Chris was having an affair.

'It came to her mind that possibly he could be cheating,' a friend, Amanda Thayer, reported to CBS News.

However, there are few relationships where some doubts do not, from time to time, arise, even if they do not relate to the fidelity of one of the partners. And her best friend and co worker at Le Vel (Shanann had also been a housing realtor) Nickole Atkinson feels differently.

'No, she did not talk about leaving him or separating. She very much loved her family and wanted to be called a family. I didn't find out they were going to separate or anything until I called Chris that morning,' she said, reflecting after her friend's death speaking to interviewers on Good Morning America. She did not, though, express surprise that Chris had been arrested. Wisdom after the event, or was she aware that there was something more to Shanann and Chris' relationship than met the eye?

On August 13th Shanann returned late from a business trip. She was collected by Nickole and driven home. Although she had no suspicions as to why, Nickole did notice that her friend was not her usual self. She seemed quiet and withdrawn. Nickole put it down to tiredness, which may well have been all that was troubling Shanann. After all, by now she was fifteen weeks pregnant, and that places inevitable strains upon a mother's body.

Further, the unborn boy had developed a small problem. Doctors had detected an irregular heartbeat, and in fact Shanann had an appointment to have her baby checked the next day.

When she failed to make that appointment, alarm bells began to ring. Such behavior was completely out of character for the committed and doting mother, and Nickole began to worry that her friend had been taken ill. She decided to go to the Watts' house and check that all was well. When she arrived there, those alarm bells began to ring even more loudly. Shanann's car was still sitting on her drive just as it had been when she had set off for her work meeting some days before.

Nickole knocked on the door, but there was no reply. She did not even hear the girls playing. Clearly, it seemed, Shanann had been taken ill. That would explain her distracted and unusual manner the night before. She considered her options, and in the end decided to call the police. Again, to undertake such a move before trying to contact Chris might be seen as surprising. No doubt, that is another fact which will come out at trial.

The police also showed concern, but they contacted Chris at work, and asked him to return home to let them in. He agreed, as would be expected from any normal, loving father and husband. The reason for any failure to answer the door, or for the girls to be playing, soon became apparent. The house was empty. There was no sign of any unrest or struggle. It was as though Shanann had simply left with the girls. The police began to talk with Chris about what could have happened, and from those discussions emerged the first concrete evidence that conditions in that relationship were nothing like as idyllic as they seemed from the outside.

That morning, said Chris, he had dropped a bombshell on his wife. As they lay in bed he announced that he wanted a separation. Whatever she might have feared in the back of her mind, it seems as though (according to Chris) she took the news as badly as could be expected. An 'emotional conversation' followed, then Shanann announced that she could not stay at their home. She needed time to think, and to get that time, she was going to a friend's house. Further, she would take Bella and Celeste with her.

The police asked for details of the friend, but here Chris' story begins to show cracks. He cannot remember the name of the friend, in fact he is not sure that his wife even offered that detail. This has to be seen as unusual; even in an emotionally charged situation such as they were facing, a person will normally identify where they plan to go, especially if children are involved. But Chris claimed he had no idea where his wife and children had gone.

Initial searches revealed nothing and within a short time the police announced Shanann and the children as officially missing. At that point they sought help from the public to trace them. The next day, Chris Watts appeared on Denver Channel 9 News, and there he pleaded for Shanann to come home, and to bring his daughters with her.

It is a strange appeal. Chris seems remarkably calm throughout; on the couple of occasions his demeanor becomes more emotional, viewers must have harbored doubts that it all seemed a little contrived. For example, he stutters over his words, and finds it hard to put together a coherent sentence.

'I have no inclination of where they're at now,' he said to the cameras. 'Every friend I have has called friends that Shannan had, who maybe I didn't know and it's just like they've vanished.'

'It's earth shattering,' he continued. 'I have no idea where they are right now. It's like a ghost town. A nightmare I can't wake up from.'

He finishes his interview by making a plea to viewers, as though hoping that Shanann might be listening somewhere. 'If they're in trouble, it's earth shattering. I need everybody back here. I need everybody safe.'

Chris Watts' performance would not win him an Oscar, or even a nomination at his local amateur dramatics society. Nobody can be really sure how they would react if their family suddenly disappeared. But certainly, Chris Watts' interview raised more questions than it answered, and any sympathy felt for him by the wider public would be tempered with doubt.

So, it was with little surprise that the very next day, August 15th, Chris made a startling admission. Shanann was, he claimed, far from the caring, loving and considerate wife she liked people to think. Instead, she was controlling, emotional and prone to fits of temper. He had hinted at such during his talk the previous day on Denver's news program. There he had likened Celeste's behavior to that of his wife, saying that she was spontaneous, full of ups and down. Of course, in a toddler such behavior is sweet and attractive, in a grown woman it is far from that.

Then, his claims took on an even more sinister tone. He had walked into their home, and the baby monitor was on, displaying the most shocking of scenes to him. He entered to see Shannan murdering Celeste. As he burst into their room, arriving too late to save his daughter, he saw the prone body of Bella lying on the floor. She too was dead. Clearly, Shanann had murdered her as well. Chris said that he flew into a rage, grabbed hold of his wife and in a momentary fit of fury, killed her. Who could blame him? Who could bear to see their children murdered by their mother? A mother who lived a dual life, who possessed a split personality in which she portrayed herself as the most caring woman to friends, to family, to the public as a whole but who, in private, was aggressive, moody and controlling.

He had no idea that she would react as such to the news that he was leaving her, and his response to seeing her actions was not right, but was, he argued, thoroughly understandable. He was the victim here. Along with his daughters, and his unborn son, but not his wife.

Quite how he tied up his ultra-calm performance on TV news the previous day with having experienced this most violent and disturbing of events just twenty four hours before that he could not say. His revelation causes astonishment among Shanann's friends and family. This is not the woman they know. Shanann is a mother who clearly loves her children and adores her husband. Chris' claim that she murdered her daughters as an act of revenge against him goes beyond the realms of possibility. Yes, she is fun loving, but she is not violent, or aggressive or prone to severe mood changes. They cannot believe the story Chris has put about.

And significantly, neither can the police.

Their suspicions are confirmed shortly afterwards when a series of discoveries are made in the extensive grounds of the petroleum company for whom he works. In a shallow grave they discover the remains of his wife. Then, in a nearby tank, the bodies of Celeste and Bella are found.

That is a very strange place to leave the bodies of daughters you claim to love. Within hours, the official charge sheet against him is made public. Chris Watts is charged with three counts of tampering with a deceased body, and three counts of first-degree murder. Two of these counts refer to his causing the death of a person under the age of twelve, while in a position of trust. The death penalty exists in Colorado, but only under very limited circumstances. One of those is for causing the death of a child under the age of twelve. Another is for knowingly ending the life of a pregnant woman. He is also charged with the unlawful termination of his wife's pregnancy.

If found guilty, Chris Watts faces a sentence of death by lethal injection.

Quite soon, it became apparent that Chris' reason for wishing to leave his wife was little, if anything, to do with his accusations about her behavior. In fact, it was something much more commonplace. He was having an affair with a co-worker. Indeed, it seems likely that he was involved in several extra marital relationships. He claimed to have told his wife that, at 5.00 am on August 13th, just three hours after she arrived back from her business trip.

The co-worker in question is still to be named, but another (again unnamed) woman has come forward to describe an affair she had with Chris Watts. He 'wasn't the kind of guy who would cuddle and watch a movie' she claimed. Rather, he had a love of rough sex.

'He would put his hands on my throat during intercourse,' she stated, having met Watts on Tinder. 'Now that I know who he is, it gives me the chills! I can't even think about it. But nothing about him alarmed me until he tried to choke me. That freaked me out. He had a rape fantasy. He was very kinky. When we had sex, it was very animalistic. He just zoned out into a different person.'

The woman alleged that thirty-three-year-old Watts would travel up to fifty kilometers to visit her in the Denver home in which she lived.

Watts may also be bi-sexual. Another anonymous alleged lover of Watts contacted the HLN host Ashleigh Banfield to claim that he had been involved in a relationship with the man accused of multiple murders.

The two had met on a dating app, MeetMe, then eventually entered into a full relationship. 'He was not out and not ready to be out as far as sexuality,' claimed the self-confessed lover. The man said that he had not been aware that Watts was married until he met his two daughters.

'He told me he was looking for a relationship in the long run. I asked why his profile said straight.' In fact, the man believes that Watts was, at the time, unsure of his sexuality. 'We had many conversations,' he alleged. 'I asked him to make sure he's not bisexual because he had two children. He told me he didn't know. At that moment he was attracted to me as a male.'

Watts purportedly went on to say that he and his wife no longer had a sexual relationship (although, his wife's pregnancy would seem to argue against that particular assertion).

Another story emerged from a woman who had met the Watts family on vacation shortly before the murders. Michele Greer was queuing to give her children a turn on a bungee trampoline at Myrtle Beach in South Carolina. She got chatting to Shanann as the Watts queued with them.

They chatted for ten minutes until the children's turn came around, when they parted company. Greer thought no more of the event until about 11 days later, when a TV news report told the story of a mother and her two daughters who had been murdered in Colorado. The photographs seemed familiar, and so Greer scrolled through her phone, looking at photos she had taken at the trampoline. There, on one captured of her own three sons, Shanann, Celeste and Bella were visible in the background.

She recalled that Chris had seemed distant and uninterested in the girls' activity. However, she finds it hard to see any truth in the claims that it was Shanann who murdered the girls.

'The mum I saw interacting with her kids is not the person who would have killed her children,' she told a local TV station. 'She was very sweet and very lovable with the girls. It was all about the girls. She told me she was expecting. She was very happy. She was very engaged with her little girls. The last thing I told her was "good luck to you". That was it.'

At the time of writing, Watts is still waiting to offer a plea against the charges levelled at him. He is locked up in the Weld County Jail, where he is separated from other inmates. The publicity surrounding the murder case is unsurprisingly intense. Therefore, for his own safety, he is being kept away from others who may wish to do him harm. At this stage, he has not been in the prison system for long enough to qualify for visitors. He is also on suicide watch, with officers checking regularly on his health and state of mind.

If Watts does enter a plea of not guilty, a major part of his defence may relate to the time since his arrest. His team have claimed much wrong doing which, if true, will have harmed his opportunity to receive a fair trial.

Defense counsel are claiming that prosecutors in Colorado have leaked sensitive information to the media. The Denver Post is claiming that Watts' team are seeking an investigation into the possibility that Weld County prosecutors, or maybe the police themselves, had taken part in releasing this sensitive information.

But to Denver criminologist Denise Mowder, the case is open and shut. Watts' motive for his crime was simply that he wanted to begin a new life with his latest lover.

Mowder, who is an associate professor of criminology and criminal justice at MSU in Denver, said: 'I think he had a vision of another life with this other woman – carefree, no responsibilities. Two children and another on the way. That's a big responsibility.'

But she is surprised that Watts did not take his own life, which is often the way when a parent kills their children. Research suggests that in about a third of cases where fathers kill their children the cause is rage, but a significant number occur as an act sparked by a desire to inflict revenge on their spouse.

Mowder believes that Watts had a plan. His willingness to make the press statement on the day his family was declared missing was a part of a scheme to get an intruder blamed for the murders. 'Somebody else did it, I'm the poor grieving father,' was the image he wished to portray.

The former prosecutor also explained that men blaming their wives for serious crimes is typical behavior of a domestic abuser. She is clear in her thinking that Watts was the perpetrator in this case.

'When he said she was the one strangling the children, I knew right then he was the one who strangled the children, because he can give all the details of what he said, and she did because he was doing it himself.'

She went on to outline some of the challenges that will face a jury, as well as the victims' family. Whatever happened next, and whether Chris Watts is found guilty of triple murder, Mowder knows the weeks, months and years ahead will be challenging for all.

'It's going to be hard on the family to hear the lies,' she said. 'And there's some secrets there, I'm afraid. It's going to be hard for the jury. It's going to be hard for the public to really understand because there is no understanding it.'

And that is, of course, the truth.

BLACK WIDOW : The True Story of DENA THOMPSON

26

BRIANNA WELLS

Dena Thompson is a woman who held power over every man that had the misfortune of falling for her charms.

Dubbed a psychopath, Dena succeeded in fooling everyone around her, including investigators, with her lies and charm for over twenty years.

Dena would post to Lonely Hearts columns and lure a steady stream of lovers and husbands into her world, eventually leaving each one emotionally and financially bankrupt.

Her first husband lost everything to her and wound up as a desperate man on the run from a mafia threat that did not exist. With one husband gone and his money spent, Thompson would go on to bigamously marry Julian Webb, a successful advertising salesman. In three short years, Mr. Webb would be found dead in his bed from an unexplainable drug overdose. Thompson's third and final husband would soon be fighting for his life when she suddenly attacked him with a bat. Still, somehow, this master manipulator would convince an entire jury that she was nothing less than the victim of abuse. No matter how many fruitless chases she sent investigators on, Thompson would not be able to keep the family members and friends of her victims from stringing the pieces together one at a time.

Her crimes were finally brought into the light of day and she would be imprisoned for her killings.

EARLY LIFE

Dena Thompson was born Dena Holmes in 1960 to a lower middle class family from Hendon, London. Her parents were named Michael and Margaret Holmes. Her father had previously worked as a prison officer but had since retired, and her mother lived as a housewife. Her childhood and teenage years held no indication of unhappiness or abuse and she graduated from school with the highest marks. Her life moved by uneventfully until, at the age of 22, she began a career with the Woolwich building society and met Lee Wyatt on a blind date set up by his cousin, Bob Reed, in 1982. On October 12th the following year, the two married in a registry office and moved into a house just below the South Downs. A small village, Dena and Lee's neighbors describe the quaint area as a "very friendly, happy place to live."

Jackie Howells, a neighbor, described the two, saying: "They were ok. You know, just ordinary neighbors when they first moved here."

Pete Howells, Jackie's husband, recalled that Mr. Wyatt was a relatively private man. "Lee kept himself to himself. You know, [polite] enough to say good morning, um, the usual things, but he was never there long enough to build up a conversation with."

Five years later, in 1987, the seemingly happy couple brought a son into the world named Darren.

Lee was an avid toy enthusiast and established the Denalee Crafts company, combining both of their names. The company would distribute hard and soft toys successfully for a time.

For extra income, Dena continued her second job working for the Woolwich building society in Arundel. Taking inspiration from the success of popular cartoon characters and the money behind merchandising, Lee worked to make his fortune by developing a soft toy character for use in cartoon films.

Their shared endeavor would prove not to be the life changing decision they thought it to be, however, when the firm went belly up and Lee was forced to allow his father-in-law to set him up with a new job at the Bedford Hotel in Brighton. Little did Lee know, that this business failure would flip a previously unseen switch in Dena's heart, hurtling her down a dark path of sex, fraud, bigamy, and murder.

Realizing that her seemingly imminent riches were gone before they began, Dena got her first taste of fraud when she began helping herself to the first installments of 26,000 pounds from the Woolwich building society. At the same time, she began to cast her eyes outward for a new man that could bring her success where she felt her current husband had failed. She soon met and began a passionate affair with Julian Webb, whom she met when he visited her office to sell advertising for the West Sussex Gazette.

Julian put forward the idea of doing a makeover using make up and clothing from local businesses in order to bring in customers. At Julian's suggestion, Dena became the model for this idea, and she was very much in love with the new work.

Julian was an active man, an avid bodybuilder and fisherman until he began a relationship with Dena. Soon, his only hobby was to please his new woman.

Peter Howells describes the moment he first saw Dena with Julian, saying: "One day, looking out the back door, [I] just happened to see Dena and another man kissing on the back doorstep, which was rather strange to say the least."

Dena loved the adrenaline rush of both stealing money and cheating on her husband. It was like a drug for her and attaining this kind of "high" would go on to dominate every action she took for the rest of her adult life.

OUT WITH THE OLD, IN WITH THE NEW

Rosemary Webb, Julian's mother, knew very little about Dena when she and Julian came to her with the announcement that they wanted to marry. Understandably, Rosemary was "a bit taken aback at the speed of this, as they'd only met last May," and they had announced their intentions in August of the same year. Only a fortnight later, wedding cards could be seen decorating the front windows of Dena's home. Neighbors were more than a little confused, since Dena Wyatt was already married. No one had seen Lee in weeks and it was as if he disappeared off the face of the earth.

Julian and Dena married on December 2nd, 1991, and Julian did not know that the marriage was bigamous.

Without Julian's knowledge, Dena had sent her first husband running for the hills only months before their marriage. Dena and Lee had signed up for the mortgage on their home together in Yapton, West Sussex. Three months later, in the year of 1991, Denawould give her husband stunning news. She claimed the two needed to separate because Lee was about to come into a large fortune, as there was allegedly a multi-million dollar deal being set up with Walt Disney over his stuffed toy named "Shaun the Leprechaun."

She told him that the mafia was now out to kill him for a cut of the money.

In order to make the lie more believable to Lee, as well as their friends and family, Dena forged letterheads from well-known toy company in the U.S. and showed them to her husband, writing up a lucrative contract that only required his signature.

Lee fell so completely for the deception that he quit his job at the Bedford Hotel.

On June 30th, a debt collector appeared at the door. Dena told her husband to run for his life while she intercepted the man. Lee would run out the back door, praying he would get away unscathed.

Fearing for his family's well-being, Lee Wyatt went on the lamb, but Dena would not allow him to fully disappear without also convincing him to write a series of letters framing himself for the Woolwich building society fraud as she continued to steal more and more money through false accounts.

In an interview taken years later, Lee was quoted saying: "She lives a life of lies and fantasy, and I was the mug who went along with it."

Lee Wyatt gave himself a new name after going on the lamb, Collin Mitchel, and sought work in the Cornish seaside resort of Newquay.

The man that eventually gave him work, David Rodd, was the manager of Carousel Amusements. He stated that Lee came in "to get away from his life in West Sussex, which was nothing strange at the time because a lot of people work for the summer, or something like that." Employees described the mysterious man as easy going and easy to talk to, happy to go out with coworkers for drinks. The job even came with a flat above the establishment that Lee rented for a place to stay. When coworkers eventually learned of his true identity much later, they were more than a little shocked.

A coworker, Mark Pope, laughed about the absurdity of such a sudden revelation, stating in an interview: "Maybe that's why when we were shouting 'Collin' he wasn't replying. We thought he might have been a little bit deaf."

For three years, Lee hid from the invisible boogeymen his cheating wife had created.

Dena, on the other end, set up shop with Julian in the house that Lee had purchased.

Lee sent most of the money he earned to his wife while he lived as a vagrant, believing that any moment his wife would call him, let him know the danger had passed, and finally tell him he could return home to the loving wife and son that awaited him. Dena, however, held no intentions of allowing him to do so, using the money he sent to fund her second wedding and even going so far as to create a gang of fictional assassins called "The G-Men" that were constantly on the hunt for their prey.

Each time Lee called home, praying that at last the "hunt" had been called off, Dena would insist he stay hidden.

Her current beau, Julian, would not be her only suitor during this time as neighbors would recount other men coming in and out of the home while her husband was away at work. There were even a few close calls in which a visitor would be leaving the home almost at the same time as Julian pulled in for lunch, something he did daily.

Christopher Cordess, a legal adviser on Dena Webb's case, had this to say of her: "She has an enormous ability to project, but this is an intense form of it. It had a sort of psychotic flavor, that is a crazy flavor, so intense that it makes people by some extraordinary mechanism -which I can't explain- has an influence over people that makes them do things which their normal selves would never do or do again."

LIES, LIES AND MORE LIES

Early on in her marriage with Julian, Dena informed her husband that she was terminally ill, and that her employer was threatening to fire her because she had taken so many days away from work due to her sickness.

Julian saw this as outrageous as Dena would look the part, acting weak and lethargic. In reality, however, Dena was being fired because 26,000 pounds were missing from accounts at the Woolwich building society, and she was being investigated for it. She claimed that her first husband, Lee, had returned and had been threatening her, blaming him for the missing money. Dena alleged that her first husband was sending her threatening letters and even secretly recorded him making threatening phone calls to her.

Dena then claimed to her neighbors, the Howells, that Lee had come to her home and raped her. The police took her false accusations seriously, and Lee Wyatt finally became the wanted man he had always wrongly believed he was.

Furious of his situation, Lee returned home whilto confront Dena while Julian was upstairs sleeping. Dena refused to explain anything and managed to turn him away. Little did she know that her web of lies had already begun to fall apart at the seams and her subsequent downfall was imminent.

In 1994, Dena took the final step in her downward spiral of darkness: murder. Detectives believe at this time Julian may have begun to discover the extent of his wife's lies before she took his life with a massive overdose of dothiepin, an anti-depressant, and aspirin hidden in his curry over the course of some days.

Julian loved curry with extra spice, a fact that Dena took advantage of to mask the bitter taste of the poison.

It was on Julian Webb's birthday, June 30th, that his devious wife first informed Julian's mother over the phone that her son had fallen ill and had in fact been sick since Tuesday, two days before.

Dena told his mother that her son had "stayed in the sun too long" and had drunk himself into a stupor, which struck his mother as strange.

She knew that her son didn't partake in alcohol.

Friends and work colleagues of Julian had their suspicions as well, as it was very unlike him to be so sick and to not check in with his loved ones. After his second day of missed work, a male co-worker called to inquire if Julian was okay.

"Oh, well, he's sick," Dena said before hanging up on the man. A number of people called the house inquiring after Julian's health, and each caller would receive a vague, fantastic story as to why he could not come to the phone or work.

At 1:30 a.m. in the morning, on Julian's birthday, Dena would ring the doorbell at the Howell residence, waking them.

She told them that she could not wake up her husband and that he was not breathing. When Dena finally called for help, her husband was long dead and rigid in his bed.

Dena presented the police with two bottles, alleging that her husband had taken an overdose of antidepressants and aspirin on purpose. This was a hard pill for his family to swallow, however, as Julian was a fitness fanatic. He never drank or even took aspirin as he was regimented toward clean living.

"I was awake when the police came 'round to tell me what had happened," Julian's mother recalled. "And I knew as soon as I saw them, before I'd spoken to them, and I heard the police car from upstairs. I just knew."

Julian Webb died of an overdose on his 31st birthday in his bed, at least two hours before an ambulance was called.

Julian's coworkers recall coming up to their work building and finding Dena sitting on the front steps a very short time after his death. She was described as moving between crying and lucidity, and the way she seemed to go between the two so quickly unnerved those that witnessed it. Dena is reported to have said in the same breath, "Julian's dead. I need to speak to someone about the insurance money." To any sane person, these two sentences could not possibly be said in the same conversation, much less the same breath, and yet here was this woman wearing a nightgown and jacket, saying just that.

Dena told the police that her husband committed suicide, but his apparent good health and happy attitude prior to his "sickness" prompted police to investigate. They would discover that the antidepressants belonged not to Julian Webb, but to Dena. Still, the pills were kept in a drawer in the kitchen, where Julian could have easily found and taken them, and thus the fact the pills belonged to Dena held little weight. Though the coroner could not confirm that he had taken the dose accidentally, there was not enough evidence to prove foul play so the medical examiner recorded an open verdict.

Wasting no time, Dena attempted to collect thirty-five thousand pounds from Julian's pension plan which was to be released in the event of his death. Julian's mother would not allow her son's murderer to get away with his life and his money, however, and she was able to quickly establish that Dena was not his next of kin as she was still legally married to her first husband.

Dena also attempted to have Julian's remains cremated, but his family and investigators were able to successfully prevent such an evidence damaging act. It would not be until her trial for attempting to murder her third husband, however, that Julian's body would be exhumed.

The funeral was held at a church on Hayling Island in Northney. Dena Webb showed up wearing a high-riding mini-skirt and a blouse that revealed her ample cleavage.

The right side of the church was packed with friends and family mourning the loss of their Julian, and to the left sat the lone figure of Dena in sexy attire. Friends and colleagues describe Dena's face as emotionless and noticed that the flowers she brought appeared to have been taken from the cemetery nearby.

Much to his family's dismay, Julian's death was eventually ruled an accidental overdose, and Dena Webb moved on in her hunt for a new man to take deadly advantage of.

The freshly widowed Dena looked for love by advertising in the personal ads, describing herself as a "bubbly blonde."

No one proved clever enough to resist her charm. Businessmen, teachers, a prison officer, and even a convicted rapist fell under her ruthless spell before she dumped them or vanished. Detectives believe Dena successfully conned her victims out of a total of a half-million pounds.

One of her victims, Robert Waite, was found and interviewed. He had worked with Dena in 1980 and, years later, suddenly received a card from her inviting him to a reunion party. He called her, and Dena invited him to dinner then seduced him.

Dena would tell Waite that Julian had died from an overdose of steroids and that her first husband, Lee Wyatt, had beaten and attacked her regularly. Waite believed her, as he had no reason not to. But when Mr. Waite began to pull away out of disinterest, Dena quickly convinced him that she was dying of a terminal illness. Wishing to help a dying woman, he promised to take her to one of her favorite places, Florida, to care for her during her last months of life. After they arrived, while the two were lying in bed at a motel, Waite woke to feel a sharp prick in his side. He became entirely sure that Dena drugged him and slept through an entire day.

Soon after, Dena left him for broke, saying she had to appear as a witness in an anti-mafia trial in New York. She was actually flying back to Britain as she was due to appear in court for defrauding the Woolwich. For three weeks, Waite was stranded. Evenually, he came back to England and on August 31st, 1995 he discovered that Dena Webb had just been convicted of fraud and sent to jail. It was revealed during this trial that Dena had falsified the alleged death threats sent to her by mail from Lee Wyatt, and even his recorded calls were scripted by her. At the time of their creation, Lee believed that he was creating them to protect his family. The police were able to conclude that Lee was in fact hundreds of miles away during the time of the thefts working in Newquay under an assumed identity, and the charges against him were dropped. Dena was released after only nine months, and she soon returned home.

A NEW MAN, ANOTHER SUCKER

Richard Thompson was just another name on the long list of pockets Dena wished to empty when he discovered her personal ad in a Lonely Hearts column. The two met and "hit it off", marrying in a Holiday Inn in Florida.

The two were forced to round up strangers, one of which was the manager of the hotel, as witnesses after Dena's supposed "friends and family" did not show.

Thompson had money and owned a home in an affluent community which Dena found to her liking. She lied and charmed Thompson, claiming a love of deep-sea fishing which was his favorite hobby.

Dena told Richard that she had won the lottery and could access the money in the States, and so the loving couple made plans to travel overseas and claim her winnings. After the trip had been finalized, Dena enthralled her new husband with ideas of becoming

"a big game ocean skipper" and opening a fishing company.

This inspired Richard to attend classes run by the U.S. Coast Guard. He passed his boating exam, a feat that did not come without a huge amount of hard work. Richard then took an early retirement, and his wife used the money to renovate his cottage in order to rent it out while they were away in Florida building their new life. The new Mrs. Dena Thompson then suggested they combine their financial assets, a suggestion that the blissfully in love Richard saw as a reasonable thing to do. He even made out his will to his wife, giving her power of attorney over his financial affairs. Not long after this, Dena allegedly asked him if their waste disposal unit might be powerful enough to crush bones. A chilling question, to be sure, but a question that Richard thought little about.

Unfortunately for Richard, his wife had a murderous surprise in store for him just one day before the couple were to leave for the States.

On that fateful night, according to Richard's testimony, his wife had promised him a wild round of rough, kinky sex which was something he eagerly accepted.

Before getting ready, Dena locked their German Shepard, Oden, away in another room. She then informed her husband that a man would be coming the following day with a green card for him, which he would then be able to use to go to Florida.

She then started to run a hot bath and told him to "get ready for some fun."

With her husband anticipating something kinky, he allowed Dena to tie up his hands and feet.

"Get ready for a night to remember," she cooed, placing a towel over his face.

Dena then picked up a baseball bat and cracked it over his head.

Once then twice for good measure.

Stunned with blood pouring into his eyes, Richard jerked and twisted his body enough to loosen the restraints on his wrists. He sat up but Dena was ready for him.

Grabbing a butcher knife from the night stand beside their bed, she stabbed him in the shoulder. Still dazed from the baseball bat hits to the head, Richard miraculously recovered and pushed Dena away.

Dena slipped on his blood on the floor. Richard seized the advantage, pushing his thumb into her eye. Dena went for the knife again but Richard pushed harder with his thumb.

"I'll put your eye through your head if you don't let go of the knife," Richard warned.

THE AFTERMATH

It would be several days after Richard fought for and won his life that the idea to check his bank accounts would suddenly come to him. A quick call had his accountant checking his assets, and sure enough, it was discovered that Dena, the woman he had grown to love, had cleaned out his bank accounts. She also made inquiries about surrendering his 89,000 pound life insurance policy and put up his house for sale without his knowledge.

"I fell for her personality," Richard said afterward. "I trusted her 100 percent."

Dena was put on trial for attempted murder and fraud, with Richard as the key witness.

She would plead not guilty and her attorney claimed it was Richard who attacked his wife, becoming violent when she told him that Florida had all been a lie, and that Dena had hit him with the bat in self-defense.

The jury fell for Dena's charm as well, acquitting her of attempted murder.

The district attorney would call the case his "the most staggering court verdict I ever had."

Dena was, however, sentenced to three years and nine months at Lewes Crown Court on fifteen counts of fraud, involving thousands of pounds that she stole from her husband Richard, as well as two other lovers. Not only had Richard been nearly murdered without warning, but now he was financially bankrupt and emotionally devastated. During the trial, Dena admitted that her husband was not the only one she had defrauded, and she was convicted to eighteen months in jail for stealing 26,000 pounds from her old employer, the Woolwich building society, by setting up fake accounts. She had also stolen 5,000 pounds from a former boyfriend.

"I had never seen such a miscarriage of justice," Richard said. "It was appalling."

Dissatisfied with the outcome of the trial, the police began an investigation into Dena's past and quickly discovered some disturbingly repetitive facts. They discovered a long train of men left destitute in the wake of the "bubbly blonde" that promised them love and companionship. They also took a second look at the fate of her late husband, Julian Webb, and the cruel lies that sent Lee Wyatt into homelessness for three years. Immediately following their discovery of Julian Webb's death and the investigation into Dena regarding his overdose, investigators reopened the case and exhumed Julian Webb's body for further examination. For six years, Dena Thompson had gotten away with murder, but the attack on her current husband would prove to be her undoing.

Forensic scientists confirmed that antidepressants caused his death, but concluded that the medication was administered over a period of time rather than all at once. This ruled out Dena's original claim of suicide and made it clear that Julian had in fact been poisoned over the course of a week. Scientists were able to prove this by examining his stomach and blood content. The last days of Julian Webb's life would have been horrific. Isolated from his friends and family, Julian would lie dying in his bed, knowing something was wrong but unable to help himself or reach out to others. All the while, Dena nursed him, likely feeding him by hand in what must have appeared to be an act of love and devotion. Instead, this monstrous psychopath was dosing him with still more and more antidepressants and aspirin.

Julian's final moments would have been filled with agony as his body shut down, with Dena's emotionless face being the last thing he would ever see.

Nine years after his untimely demise, Julian Webb's killer would finally be brought to justice. In 2003, Dena Thompson received life, with a minimum of sixteen years, for murder.

FINALLY...

Dena Thompson was a master manipulator of people, with one husband murdered, another almost murdered, and a third on the run and penniless.

The Recorder of London, Michael Hyam, is quoted saying to Mrs. Thompson that her crimes were "utterly ruthless and without any pity. Nothing can excuse you for the wickedness of what you did."

Immediately after the conviction, UK investigators put together a large scale search for any and all of Mrs. Thompson's previous victims with the fear that they had a serial killer on their hands. The search took investigators and Interpol across the length of Europe to Bulgaria, where Dena had been a regular visitor throughout the late 1970s and early 1980s. One Bulgarian boyfriend by the name of Stoyan Kostov was never found, and the fear is that he was an early victim of Dena who was no referred to as the "Black Widow." How did she make her way to Bulgaria?

Dena was an avid gymnast at a young age, although she never chose to compete, and her father, Michael Holmes, was highly involved in the sport. This is allegedly how Mrs. Thompson's Bulgarian connections were made.

Inspector Martyn Underhill felt a certain sense of urgency when searching for Mr. Kostov (last known address: 27 K.D. Avramov Street, Svishtov), but was unable to find the man.

"We cannot rule out the possibility that other partners have been injured in some way," Inspector Underhill said.

Dena visited Bulgaria for several years, with her gymnastics connections said to be her reason. Much mystery hangs over these visits and the still missing Kostov, and it is suggested that Dena's murderous ways began long before she ever met Julian Webb. If Kostov is indeed Dena Thompson's first victim, he could be the only person on earth capable of shedding light on what turned Dena towards a life of crime.

The investigation came to an eventual end, however, when no solid evidence could be found on any murders prior to Julian Webb. Some, including a UK journalist named Adrian Gatton, believe that there is much more to the Bulgarian story than could be found by police. It is suggested that the operation carried out by Interpol and West Yorkshire police was done half-heartedly, as they may never have visited Bulgaria.

There are likely many unnamed men made victims by Dena Thompson's grandiose lies, but they might feel too embarrassed to come forward and identify themselves. It is proven that she stole from a dozen different men, but police believe the number to be much larger. Dena Thompson maintains her innocence, and her most recent appeal against conviction has failed.

In 2007, she was sentenced to a minimum of sixteen years in prison.

GOLD DIGGER VIRGINIA LARZELERE

42

SAMANTHA RUE

Virginia Larzelere: Incarcerated and spared the electric chair

Mid-afternoon shots rang out in the middle of a suburban dental clinic almost 27 years ago. A frantic call was received by emergency dispatch. The call was made by the wife of the slain dentist yelling down the line for assistance to save her husband's life, following a fatal gunshot wound to the chest.

March 8, 1991 was the day that changed Virginia Larzelere's life forever. The cold-blooded murder of her dentist husband Norman Larzelere sparked off a chain of events that culminated in her lifelong incarceration. Although it could be proven that she never pulled the trigger on her husband, the prosecution successfully argued that she was the mastermind behind the crime. Police investigating the crime scene discovered that as Norman lay dying in a pool of blood he mumbled, "Was that Jason?"

Jason was his son, adopted when he had married Jason's mother.

The investigation would result in a bizarre set of confessions that implicated Virginia Larzelere in the murder for money case. Psychiatric and hearsay evidence pointed to the motive of death to be avarice and a psychopathic manipulation of men throughout her life. Although Virginia's death sentence was commuted to life in 2008, she asserts she is still innocent to this day.

The Crime: Murder at midday, March 8, 1991

The masked killer silently entered through the back door of the dentist's surgery, with a sawed-off shotgun held by his side. His mission was to kill Norman Larzelere, possibly for the life insurance money in some sort of deal with Virginia. The sound of footsteps alarmed Norman as he had not heard anyone enter through the door.

During the trial, Dr Larzelere was reported to have said, "Who's there?" The other occupants of the office at the time were his wife Virginia and the state's witness, Kristen Palmieri who barely looked up when Norman went into the corridor to find out what the disturbance was.

Testimony provided in the first murder hearing alleged that upon seeing a gunman in the shady office corridor, he yelled, "No!" and ran back into the office slamming his office door behind him. The gunman who was in close pursuit was able to pull the trigger once, shattering through the door and hitting the doctor's chest. He subsequently died at the scene from a combination of chest trauma causing a pneumothorax (collapsed lung) and fatal blood loss.

His wife, Virginia, rushed to his side and yelled for someone to call 911. The report from the ambulance dispatcher subsequently reported that Virginia yelled to the 911 dispatcher, "Someone just came in and shot my husband! Somebody shot my husband!"

As Norman's life seeped away, she cradled him, crying. The witness alleged that he asked Virginia, "Where's Jason? Was that Jason?" By the time the police and ambulance had arrived, the gunman had fled, leaving behind a trail of devastation and turmoil. Just as he had sneaked into the clinic without being detected that fateful afternoon, as he was able to leave with none of the witnesses able to positively identify him.

The question, "Was that Jason?" uttered by the dying man, formed the basis of an investigation, where the prosecution's case pinning the murder of Dr Norman Larzelere on Virginia's biological son, Jason.

Betrayal, Lies, Manipulation

Piecing together the various players in this shocking murder for money was the task of Detective Dave Gamell. His first major lead came from the confession of Steve Heidle who had called the detective in May to reveal his hand at disposing of the murder weapon. He claimed that he had been directed by Virginia to clean the weapon in muriatic acid and then bury it in concrete.

Heidle claimed that he was aided in his endeavours by the witness Kristen Palmieri, who like himself, was employed by the slain victim's wife, Virginia Larzelere. Both of them gave statements saying that Virginia had blackmailed them into doing terrible things. Heidle also confessed to knowing about a plan to kill Norman for his life insurance and he alleged that she paid her son Jason $200,000 to kill his adopted father and benefactor.

Heidle, like many others that were unveiled during the investigation, was used as a pawn of Virginia Palmieri to assist in the hiding of evidence. Heidle spent hours with Gamell and provided a lot of useful evidence, not just about disposing the weapons but also about the family dynamics at play that led to the murder being committed by Jason.

According to the state prosecutors, the main motive for killing the well-respected and loved dentist was to bank the payout from Norman's recent increase in life insurance, which had been in place just prior to his untimely death.

Heidle claimed that Virginia had an insatiable appetite for men and money. He also claimed she lived a life filled with drugs and crime all of which made him intimidated to stand up to her. He told Detective Gamell, that if she could get her husband killed in broad daylight, then he feared for his own life if he did not do as instructed. He agreed to hide the evidence and buried the gun deep in the waters of Pellicer Creek.

That same afternoon following Heidle's confession, Kristen Palmieri was called for questioning. She corroborated Heidle's account of the events, telling the detective that she knew that hiding the weapons was wrong. She said that she had never believed that Jason could have been the murderer but subsequently Jason had confessed to her that he had been forced to kill his father at Virginia's behest.

Sure enough, police divers uncovered a plastic container with a rusted shotgun embedded in concrete in Pellicer Creek. In exchange for turning state's witness, Heidle and Palmieri were granted immunity from further prosecution.

Following this significant piece of evidence, Virginia Larzelere was caught and arrested by police the following day. It was said she was attempting to flee from Edgewater with a lot of cash and jewellery in her purse. Detective Gamell had years of experience in homicide investigations and claims he could detect her fake mourning. "I've dealt with a lot of murders and a lot of deaths," Gamell said. "And you know when someone mourns legitimately and when someone's overacting. That's how she seemed."

Gold Digging and Incest: the prosecution's case

As the state's case against Jason and his mother unfolded, it was Heidle's statements to police that provided ample motive for the crime. Heidle claimed that he'd overheard a conversation between Jason and Virginia where she had said that she'd increased the life insurance policy and forged his signature. Dr Larzelere had no suspicions of his wife's dark intentions. Heidle's sworn statement reads, "She said she's [forged] all of Norman's legal documents and it was no big deal." Evidence presented in court revealed that prior to the murder, there had been an increase on the value of the life insurance from $1 million to $2.1 million. Furthermore, a few weeks before the murder, it appeared that his will had been amended to favor his wife. Previously, she was not listed as a sole benefactor.

The trial was a field day for sensationalist journalists who reported on the case. There were many scandalous angles to report. Virginia had already been involved in an embezzlement scheme some years before. Although the charges had been dropped, it was clear that the many people in her life (such as the key witness Heidle) did not like her. It was argued that Virginia was a heartless gold digger who had a long history of manipulating all the men in her life in order to get better resources and status.

While Norman had been dearly loved in Edgewater, it was the belief of many in the small town, that Virginia's arrival in his life was a targeted and calculated move by her. She was a ruthless femme fatale who saw the married dentist as an easy mark. Norman had divorced his wife soon after beginning an affair with Virginia and they married within two months of the divorce being finalized.

Heidle was the key witness and he gave evidence throughout the trial of many instances that implicated Virginia with the murder. Allegations were that Norman Larzelere's life insurance policy and will were forged were denied by Larzelere's defence attorney, Jack Wilkins.

Wilkins was an attorney who loved representing members of the rich party crowd to which Virginia belonged. He claimed that it was great to represent this echelon of drug-taking socialites, as they always paid in cash. Wilkins seemed more like *Breaking Bad's* Saul Goodman, flamboyantly representing drug dealers and winning on minor technicalities.

Wilkins was more a party boy than a lawyer, and while he did have credibility in winning some prominent cases, he lacked the experience to deal with serious forensic evidence. Although he won a prominent civil rights case permitting a small town cinema to sell pornographic movies, he was simply out of his depth in a murder trial.

Virginia's poor choice of lawyer was to seal her fate. Wilkins was a dreadful choice to represent her as he'd admitted, "I'd never done a capital murder case before." During Larzelere's appeal case, evidence was tendered to the court to show that Wilkins had a very serious substance abuse problem, with daily use of vodka, cocaine and methamphetamines. Wilkins did try to turn down the case, but Virginia insisted on retaining him.

The relatively inexperienced and often inebriated Wilkins had to go up against the surgical-like precision of Special Prosecutor Dorothy Sedgwick's argumentative style. Appointed by the District Attorney, Sedgwick was chosen for her assassin-like instincts to win at all costs. She ran a vicious case against Virginia calling into question the background of the accused.

It was only in the subsequent appeal hearings against the death sentence that many important facts about Virginia's early life were brought to light. Much of the blame for this apparent miscarriage of proper judicial process can be laid at Wilkins' feet. Even Sedgwick was on the record commenting that a decent defence lawyer would have called witnesses to refute some of the state's evidence. Wilkins never sought the opinion of a psychiatrist nor any other expert to take the stand on Virginia's behalf.

The multi-generational level of neglect and sexual misconduct towards children was the key to the prosecution case. Court reports show that under psychiatric questioning, it was clear that as a child growing up, Virginia believed that sexual behavior with family members was the norm. This allowed the prosecutor to paint Virginia as a ruthless killer. In other words, if she was a murderer, being an incestuous murderer made it all the more salacious and perhaps believable to the jury who ultimately convicted her of the murder of Dr Norman Larzelere.

Under Sedgwick's direction, the jury was directed to focus on Virginia's apparently insatiable appetite for men and money as the primary motivation for the murder plot. Sedgwick presented psychiatric evidence to prove that Virginia had a personality disorder which caused her pathological love of money and control.

In the trial, Virginia was successfully portrayed as a manipulative woman with psychopathic tendencies who seduced her son Jason to murder his father, in order to benefit from the life insurance claim. She then used money and blackmail to gain the loyalty of people such as Heidle and Palmieri and her own children.

The state was unable to convict Jason and he was acquitted in 1992 as there was insufficient evidence to place him at the scene of the crime that fateful March day in 1991. However Virginia's guilty verdict and death sentence stayed. It was always clear that she did not murder her husband by her own hand, but suspicions remain as to her collusion due to the circumstantial evidence

How did it come to this?

Virginia grew up in the 1950s in a small town called Lake Wales, 60 miles south of Orlando, Florida. She was the oldest of four daughters all living with their Mom and Dad in a three bedroom bungalow in the working class part of the town. Both of her parents worked in a local juice company called Donald Duck.

Dr Mosman, the psychiatrist giving evidence in the appeal case told the court that she had confided to him that her father, "Pee-Wee" Antley, was a strong dictator whose moods ruled the house of women. It was noted he was a huge drinker who sexually abused each of his daughters (and subsequently Virginia's own children Jessica and Jason). In an interview with the Miami New Times in 2013, Virginia said, "sexual abuse doesn't only happen in poor households, does it?"

Virginia's younger sister, Peggy, testified that Virginia took more of the sexual abuse from their father in an attempt to spare her younger sisters. The abuse would gave birth to a burden of silence, of not being able to confide in people outside the family or to get any help for them or their mother. Mosman revealed to the court that the father was, "a chronic alcoholic, sitting on the porch drinking daily, with no outside hobby or social interests."

Virginia left home at the age of seventeen but the scars of abuse never left. Having been a victim of abuse from as young as the age of three, the emotional and sexual trauma stayed with her and influenced her outlook on life and on men. Virginia knew that the best way to survive was to use men to gain access to the wealth that she needed to feel free from her demons.

Her success at attracting many men (she was married three times by the time she was in her early 30s) came about because she was able to use her looks and sexual conduct to acquire goods and status throughout her life. Even Virginia's daughter Jessica (from her first marriage to Harry Mathis), said that the child abuse she had suffered led her to be ruthless and impulsive. Jessica has stated in an interview some years ago that, 'My mother is a very intelligent woman, who had looks which she used to her advantage." The state's case relied on this aspect of her love of the high life and of sexual promiscuity to draw the sketch of her as a ruthless gold-digging murderer.

The entire prosecution case was based on Heidle's voluntary testimony, which painted Virginia as the product of a dysfunctional and incestuous family. It was alleged that her exposure to serious childhood abuse and trauma led to her manipulative and ruthless tendencies. However, no psychiatrist was ever called by the defence to undertake an evaluation of her mental state.

Virginia's teen marriage

In Lake Wales where Virginia was growing up, she did not have any friends. This is because her domineering father felt the need to protect his filthy secret from authorities so visitors were restricted from visiting the home.

Virginia attended and graduated from Lake Wales High school and immediately fled home to marry Harry Mathis when she was only 17 years old. Soon after the marriage, she fell pregnant with Jason and then Jessica. Experts say that people often people who have dysfunctional parents often choose dysfunctional partners, and this certainly appears to be the case with Virginia.

She was trapped as a young mom, from a dysfunctional background now living with an abusive husband. Harry Mathis beat his wife and son Jason, as evidenced in the police records. Virginia divorced him in 1978, determined to be as far away from his abuse as possible, and wanting a new life for her two young children, Jason and Jessica. Instead of seeing her getting away from Harry as a triumph against abuse, the prosecutor used this to demonstrate that Virginia 'burned through' husbands. The prosecutor even used the fact that she wished for her abusive ex-huband's death as evidence of her murderous intent for Norman.

However, despite the various setbacks, abuse and domestic violence there remained in Virginia evidence of a clear determination to not only survive but thrive. Once she had escaped her parental home of horror, she went into another dysfunctional marriage for a brief period. It is also a fact that she had turned to substances to numb the emotional pain from a young lifetime of abuse. She was clearly not the most stable woman in Edgewater, but she was a survivor.

Leaving Mathis started her love of freedom, and of the partying good life that has been portrayed through documentaries about the case.

Socialite in the making

Having been divorced at the age of 25, and with two young children in tow, Virginia was clearly on a mission to find a man that would replace their biological father as a role model in her life. Being denied a good role model of appropriate masculinity, she was easily distracted by the promises of various men simply looking for a woman to bed. However, she was also hungry for money and status but preferred freedom to being tied to a man It appears that her main goal since leaving home at 17 had been to free herself from the control of a man.

Her hunger for a better life, even being married three times before she was 32, demonstrates a decision to turn away from the cycle of abuse that her mother had endured. Virginia's mother stayed by her husband's side through the mistreatment and abuse of all of his daughters. In a sense, her mother colluded with him by permitting the abuse to be perpetuated, child after child. Her misplaced loyalty for, and fear of, her husband kept her at his side.

Virginia's drive to be different from her passive mother showed her adventurous spirit, her impulsiveness and her keen business sense. By the mid-1980's she had worked her way up to being the president of a construction company based in the little town of Edgewater, a seaside town, two hours north of her hometown, Lake Wales. Although Edgewater was still a very small and isolated town, she had successfully changed her fortunes. Her financial success had become like a drug It made her feel good, and the more she did of it, the better she felt.

Her stars changed completely in 1985 due to the happenstance of a dental appointment where she was to meet the love of her life. It was in Dr Norman Larzelere's dental surgery that love was born. Virginia claims that from that first meeting she knew he was 'the one'. The feelings were clearly mutual, as the already married dentist quickly divorced his wife so that he could make a life for Virginia and her children. He embraced Jason and Jessica as his own and officially adopted them when they married.

"There was nothing but love in that household," fhe family's housekeeper Juanita Washington said. "Nothing but love." Upon their marriage, the newlyweds Virginia and Norman promptly moved into a mansion in a prestigious uptown area. The home had previously housed all sorts of people from the higher echelons of society including congressional representatives and bank presidents. By all accounts, despite the differences in their social standings and backgrounds, they seemed to be deliriously happy and to be true soul mates.

Storm clouds over paradise

However, things started to get a bit difficult the following year as Virginia's business went bankrupt amid allegations of embezzlement. Settling out of court, all criminal charges were dismissed. Around this time, her teenage son Jason was getting a bit out of hand, as teenagers in blended families often do.

Jason was a known party boy in the local Orlando gay club scene. He also befriended drag queens and seemed to have inherited his biological father's love of beating women."He threw me down the stairs and broke my ribs by kicking me over and over again," his sister Jessica recalled.

"I had told my dad that Mom was cheating on him with a patient of his." Jason staunchly defended his mother and allegations of her sexual appetites together with her son's strong filial devotion was a source of gossip surrounding their potentially incestuous relationship.

Virginia never denied her sexual liaisons with several men, two of whom testified that she had asked them to 'get rid' of Norman. It was clear that whatever their relationship was in public, Norman was unable to control his headstrong and hard-partying wife. Some of the testimonies only came to light when these men of low character asked to be paid to testify, making them barely credible.

No friends to testify on Virginia's behalf

With the public salivating upon every salacious fact, it was fair to say that Virginia and Jason Larzelere were convicted in the court of public opinion before the jury delivered its 5-7 guilty verdict for Virginia. Jason was subsequently acquitted due to the flimsy evidence by a disgruntled employee (Heidle) being the sole evidence in the case. Subsequent hearings brought to light the fact that the lone gunman that fateful day was not Jason, as Heidle had conveniently framed him for the murder. As Heidle had been given immunity from prosecution, many speculate that he tainted the stories about Virginia to protect himself and that it was he who murdered Larzelere. He committed suicide in 1999.

The allegations that Virginia was the mastermind who had her husband killed in cold blood to collect on his significant life insurance were presented but never successfully refuted. Her defence lawyer did not call any witness to the stand to testify on her behalf. A lifetime of alienation from meaningful relationships robbed her of this comfort. Her childhood of abuse and neglect impaired her ability to make and sustain meaningful and enduring friendships.

Her death sentence was overturned in 2008 though she remains incarcerated in the Homestead Correctional Institution, a 65-year-old widow, and she still maintains her innocence.

HUSBAND KILLER : THE TRUE STORY OF MICHELLE HALL

54

TORI BAKER

It's never easy being a member of a blended family. There's a certain understanding that comes along with a second or third marriage – especially one involving children – that there is going to be a fundamental need for combined effort, tolerance and compromise.

When Michelle Garner remarried for what would be the third and last time, family and friends believed she had finally found happiness after reconnecting with an old high-school flame.

John Brittson "Britt" Hall, an aircraft mechanic and home builder, had known his own fair share of heartache; he was recently divorced when he found his old high school girlfriend, Michelle, on an online dating web site.

Britt Hall and Michelle Garner first met in 1986 while attending high school in Newnan, GA. The two briefly dated before Michelle Hall graduated in 1987.

"They both were in the popular clique," forensic psychologist Robert Brion said. "Britt was a baseball player that all of the girls had a crush on. Michelle was popular herself, very outgoing with a lot of friends."

The parents of Britt and Michelle were friends as well but they didn't consider the dating relationship between Michelle and Britt to be a serious one. After graduation, Michelle would move away and she would marry a man named Rusty Hart. The couple would have two daughters until their divorce in 1996.

The single mom worked as a dental assistant to support her daughters. Times were tight until 1999 when she met and married Steve Davis.

"Steve Davis was a businessman," Brion said. "He was divorced himself with a daughter of his own. He met Michelle and quickly fell for her charms as she could come across as a very warm and caring person. He asked her to marry him after about a year of dating."

Michelle would become pregnant during the union and give birth to her third daughter, Alyssa.

Unfortunately, her second marriage met the same fate as her first and within a few years, the couple had filed for divorce, citing irreconcilable differences.

Britt did well for himself after high school, becoming an airline mechanic for Delta Airlines. He made good money with Delta until they laid him off. He then went into business with his father in home construction until ultimately returning back to Delta after they had a rehire.

His marriage started to fail, however. His first wife cited that Britt had "mental problems" and filed for divorce, stating that the marriage was "irretrievably broken."

"Britt's first wife would take him to court at least six to eight times a year after their divorce," Brion said. "He was depressed and the court visits weren't helping."

His divorce would coincide with Michelle's impending divorce with Steve Davis. Her divorce with Davis was a particularly nasty one and Britt could sympathize. They would reconnect over a dating website.

In the midst of her own divorce, Garner was happy to find love again with Britt Hall as they rekindled old flames. Shortly after reconnecting, Britt invited Michelle over for Sunday lunch with his family, and all seemed well for the couple.

"Michelle did mention to Britt's family that she was going through some difficult times with her divorce," Brion said. "She was cheerful throughout but hinted that the custody battles she was going through were quite serious."

Little did Britt Hall's family know that their excitement would soon be turned to devastation; a tragedy that would make national headlines and be detailed in various murder documentaries.

THE BRADY BUNCH

Ronald Hall, Britt's father was all to happy to have Michelle back in his son's life. At least at first.

"We visited and talked," Ronald said. "And she came in and was just as happy as she ever was," he said.

It wasn't long before Britt Hall's romance with Garner turned more serious, and the two tied the knot in September of 2006. The new marriage was an adjustment, to say the least. Britt had three children from his previous marriage and Michelle Hall had three of her own children as well. The blended family of eight was now living in Britt Hall's town home.

"You can imagine how tight the living quarters were," Brion said. "But Michelle's girls really took to their new stepfather. They became comfortable enough to call him 'Dad'."

Britt wanted a bigger home and decided to build a large home with the help of his father. The men paid for contractors to pour concrete and establish the foundation, but father and son built the majority of the house by hand.

"People didn't know where the couple were getting the money to build the house," Brion said. "But Britt did most of the work himself after the foundation was laid. So he was able to save a lot of money when it came to sweat equity. That's a testimony to how badly he wanted the marriage between he and Michelle to work out."

When all was said and done, Britt and Michelle Hall were the proud owners of a beautiful 4100 square foot home on ten acres, the perfect place to spend the rest of their lives together. The brand new house boasted vaulted ceilings, granite counter tops, and a finished basement. The construction would prove to be a house of cards, however, as things were brewing underneath the surface.

Michelle didn't have much luck with her two previous marriages, and although individual accounts may vary, her two former husbands are both to have reported being abused by Michelle during the course of their marriage.

Michelle never had a firm grasp on her emotions and didn't handle anger well. These character flaws would not bode well for her life with

Britt. Dealing with both partners' ex-spousal issues including custody and visitation, Michelle and Britt found themselves tinkering on the edge of divorce after a few months into their marriage.

"The way Britt and Michelle handled their issues were different," said family friend Sue Mathis. "Michelle was quicker to speak her mind and a lot of times, Britt just wanted her to try to gain a little bit more self-control."

Dealing with his own ex-wife and their similar divorce problems, Britt Hall was also facing his own internal battles with depression. Although he wasn't often the instigator in their frequent arguments, he was known to fervently engage in the verbal conflicts. While this certainly wasn't conducive to a happy and fruitful marriage, Britt Hall made it clear to friends he would not give up on his family and the life he had built.

The next couple of years came with continued stress, intensified by financial worries after the Halls realized they had gotten too far deep in debt as a result of building their dream home. Notices of foreclosure, liens on the house, and over-extensions were haunting the couple and causing both spouses to hit a breaking point.

On July 30, 2008, it was another typical tense day in the Hall household. Friends say Britt Hall, already aggravated due to a landscaper failing to complete a job on time, went to the store to pick-up hot dogs for a family get-together.

"Hey hon," Britt said as he called his wife. "How many hot dogs do you think I should get-"

"Count how many damn people are here," Michelle snapped. "That's how much you should get."

This would be the snide comeback that would break the straw in Britt's back. He grew tired at her constant bickering and baiting. When he came home that evening, a fight would ensue.

Michelle's youngest daughter, Alyssa, was in the living room watching television as her mother vacuumed to prepare for the company soon arriving. When Britt Hall told Alyssa to turn the TV down, another argument between the couple ensued and Hall immediately told her daughter to go upstairs to her bedroom and not come out until she was called.

There are only two individuals who know the details of what followed on that evening, and only one of them lived to tell. When all was said and done, Britt would be dead and Michelle would be charged with murder.

The 911 call came in at 8:02 p.m. by a frantic Michelle who told dispatchers that her husband had tried to kill her and commit suicide.

"He shot at me, and we were fighting to get it," Michelle told dispatchers regarding the weapon. She said she heard the gun go off twice. Seconds later, she told dispatchers her husband was turning blue.

When police arrived, Britt Hall was dead and had three noticeable gunshot wounds to his body: one on his left arm, one on his right thigh, and a close-range shot to his chest. Michelle Hall, bruised, scraped and covered in blood, told first responders the same story she had told dispatchers: her suicidal husband had tried to kill her before turning the gun on himself.

Prior to further investigation, deputies on the scene immediately called Britt Hall's parents and told them their son had committed suicide. The Halls refused to believe the news.

"Things just seemed to be going too good at this time in his life for him to have done that," said his mother, Charlene Hall. "I knew he didn't kill himself; I knew for a fact that didn't happen."

It didn't take long for police to begin seeing the crime scene a little differently than Michelle had described. Blood splatter and numerous bullet holes covered the downstairs bedroom, and a trail of blood led into the bathroom where Britt Hall's lifeless body now lay. If this was a suicide, there sure was a struggle beforehand.

Investigators gave Michelle the opportunity to explain the scene. She told how an argument between the couple turned violent when Britt

Hall threw her onto the bed. He immediately went into the study and she followed him.

Then she noticed the gun on the computer desk.

Knowing her husband was battling depression, she said she immediately became concerned with his safety, worried that he may use the gun to harm himself.

Michelle stated that she instinctively dove for the gun, and that's when Britt Hall reached for it as well and the two began struggling for possession.

After both Michelle and her husband lost control of he gun, she quickly picked up the weapon and began shooting rounds into the walls and floor in an effort to unload the gun.

In the hall, Britt Hall caught up with her and that's when she said he threatened to kill her. In yet another entanglement of an attempt for control of the gun, Michelle said the gun accidentally went off. This shot punctured Britt Hall's thigh, and that's when Hall claimed she went to call for help.

Britt Hall began crawling into the bathroom, unable to walk and calling out her name for help. When she approached him, gun in hand, she said he grabbed the pistol from her, put it to his chest, and pulled the trigger.

The problem with her story, however, was that most suicides don't entail multiple gunshot wounds. Additionally, the manner in which the fatal shot was delivered raised eyebrows for investigators.

"I've worked many suicides in my career, and I've never worked a suicide that I can remember where a man had shot himself in the chest," Lt John Lewis said.

Furthermore, the gunshot wound on Britt Hall's chest had no signs of charring or burning around the entry wound, signs which usually indicate a self-inflicted wound.

Britt Hall also had a shattered elbow and a bullet hole in his left arm. Three different shots, all which led investigators to believe they weren't being told the whole story.

Michelle did her best to persuade the investigative team to believe her story, but her story changed upon being brought to the station for questioning. While at first she claimed the two struggled for control over the gun, she then claimed Britt Hall was never actually in possession of the gun at all.

Coupled with the evidence at the crime scene and her story's inconsistencies, Michelle was charged the next morning with the murder of her husband.

Crucial to the prosecution's case was the testimony of Michelle's youngest daughter, Alyssa, who was in the home during the shooting. Police brought the 8-year-old in for questioning immediately following the incident and she clearly stated she heard her step-father pleading with her mother to "put the gun down," she said. Alyssa would ultimately testify in her mother's trial in 2009.

Facing charges of malice murder and aggravated assault, Michelle vehemently denied killing her husband. She insisted that he died of a self-inflicted gunshot wound after threatening suicide and fighting with her over the .38 caliber revolver.

The fight that evening was par for the course, she said. The two regularly got into verbal and physical altercations, and their marriage was falling apart due to financial stress. They would also constantly fight over ex-spouses, custody and visitation regarding the six children. Although there were no police reports relating to any domestic altercations in the home before, family and friends knew things weren't okay on the home front.

"Britt would spend several nights driving to work calling me and saying 'I don't know what to do.' He would have done everything in his power to save his marriage, even if it was not worth saving. He was terrified of failure," said Mathis.

One of the first fights that turned physical in front of the family was in November 2006, when Britt Hall's eldest daughter came into the room to find Michelle Hall unconscious. Her father quickly ushered her out of the room and told her not to worry about it. The next couple of years only brought more trouble due to the same old problems and Britt's alleged mental illness.

Britt was prescribed three different types of medication for depression at the time of his death, police confirmed.

But the physical evidence did not add up to suicide. Initially, the Georgia Bureau of Investigation estimated the fatal gunshot to have been fired from around 18-24 inches away. This is not consistent with suicide, detectives argued. While many victims of mental illness fall prey to suicide each year, the facts must add up. In this case, they did not.

If convicted, Michelle was facing life in prison.

In September of 2009, testimonies were heard by Alyssa Davis, as well as responding officers Capt. Tony Grant and Sgt. Freddy Cox, about what they saw and heard on the night of the shooting.

Cox testified that Hall's appearance was "consistent with someone who'd been in a physical altercation" and that Hall had bruises, scrapes and blood on her neck and forehead as well as blood on her hands and a knot on her elbow.

During his testimony, Grant stated he immediately noticed that Hall's face was red and she had what appeared to be gun-shot residue on her hand, even though she was stating her husband had committed suicide.

There were multiple bullet holes throughout the downstairs of the home when police arrived on the scene, Grant testified. Two bullets were recovered from Britt Hall's body and three more were found in the house.

Grant said a blood pattern analysis showed blood spatters of 90 degrees in the downstairs quarters outside of the bathroom, proof that Britt Hall crawled into the bathroom after being wounded.

Defense Attorney Mike Kam said that while in no uncertain terms would he call the key ear witness a liar, her age and her location during the shooting did not make for the most reliable testimony.

"She was eight; she didn't see anything, she clearly got some of the facts confused." Kam said in an interview. "She's not someone who is used to being asked questions in formal interview settings. Who knows what she remembered, or what happened?"

Additionally, Kam indicated that Michelle certainly didn't fit the description of a murderer. Outside of two divorces, Hall had no criminal record. She was law-abiding citizen, with nothing in her background which would give the assumption she was capable of murder, he said.

But the jury had heard enough. On September 25, 2009, Michelle Hall was found guilty on all counts in the death of her husband Britt.

Not long after her conviction, Hall's attorneys filed a motion for a new trial, citing trial court errors. Coweta County Superior Court Judge Jack Kirby denied the motion and the defense attorneys took the case to the Supreme Court.

On September 22, 2010, the Supreme Court of Georgia upheld the conviction, despite Hall's defense's argument that the trial court erred by admitting similar transaction evidence and prior consistent statements.

Hall's defense stated that testimony from both of her ex-husbands that she was verbally and physically abusive were inadmissible because they were not "sufficiently similar" to establish proof of the crimes for which she was charged, according to the opinion of the Supreme Court. It also stated that "in cases of domestic violence, prior incidents of abuse against family members or sexual partners are more generally permitted because there is a logical connection between violent acts against two different persons with whom the accused had a similar emotional or intimate attachment."

The opinion also added that the fifteen and thirteen-year lapses of time between her ex-husband's allegations of abuse to the alleged shooting of her husband did not require exclusion of evidence.

"Given that the similar transaction evidence reflects appellant's behavior towards prior spouses, we conclude that any prejudice from the age of these prior incidents was outweighed by the probative value of the evidence under the particular facts of this case and the purpose for which the similar transactions were offered."

Eighteen months later, however, Michelle retained a new attorney who filed a habeas corpus petition, stating Michelle was given ineffective legal counsel by Kam during her trial in 2009. Senior Judge Robert B. Struble presided over the hearing and determined that Hall was in-fact entitled to a new trial. Struble agreed that Kam, Hall's trial attorney, was "ineffective and fell below the minimum guarantee of representation under the constitution," a press release said.

While Michelle may have been looking forward to another chance at redemption, The Attorney General's Office quickly announced their plans to appeal the habeas corpus ruling to the Georgia Supreme Court.

In a press release on March 30, 2012, Coweta County District Attorney Peter John Skandalakis expressed his respectful disapproval of the court's ruling and that in stating Kam was ineffective for representation, "the court erroneously applied the wrong standard under the law."

Skandalakis said he was optimistic that the Supreme Court will conclude that Hall had a legally sufficient defense and that her conviction would be upheld after review of the appeal.

On January 22, 2013, the Supreme Court found Hall's convictions to be fair and just, denying insufficient representation during her 2009 trial. According to the court summary, the Supreme Court concluded that the habeas corpus petition did not conduct proper legal analysis to determine the effectiveness of Hall's defense.

The opinion references Strickland v. Washington, a 1984 Supreme Court case in which it determined that to be granted a new trial, a defendant must show that it was due to insufficient performance by defense that the defendant was found guilty.

Michelle's argument for her habeas corpus petition was that "if she were in the same room when her young daughter was questioned, she could have assisted her attorney by prompting him with specific information," the court says in its opinion. However, it was determined during the habeas hearing that any information she would have portrayed to her attorney was already known information to both parties. "As such, Hall has failed to show actual prejudice, and her claim of ineffective assistance of counsel should have been rejected," the opinion said.

Today, Michelle Hall remains in a Coweta County prison.

Since her conviction, Michelle's ex-husbands have been given full custody of her three respective daughters.

She won't be eligible for parole until 2039. She will be 70 years old.